OUTSIDE THE SCHOOL OF THEOLOGY

OUTSIDE THE SCHOOL OF THEOLOGY

OUTSIDE THE SCHOOL OF THEOLOGY

OUTSIDE THE SCHOOL OF THEOLOGY

T e r i   Z i ƥ ʃ

TSUNAMI INC.

Acknowledgments

Some of these poems appeared originally in *Calapooya Collage, The Collegian, The Fishtrap Anthology, The Gadfly, Kinesis, the kore, Nature's Advocate, Northern Lights, Oregon East, Rain City Review, Signs of the Times, Storm Warnings, Talking River Review, The Temple* and *What's Up.*

The author wishes to thank Trevor Dorland, Ann Hoxsey, Darinda Huntley, Lisa Krueger and Kari Zipf for their help with the design and production of this book. The Artist Trust provided confirmation, encouragement and financial support. Rich Wandschneider and the people at Fishtrap gave me a place to be a writer. Special thanks to David Reimer whose friendship and editorial advice have improved my life and particularly this book, beyond measure.

© 1997 by Teri Zipf

Design: Trevor Dorland

Zipf, Teri
Outside the School of Theology
First Edition 1997

1997
Library of Congress: 97-60378
ISBN 0-9644440-4-6

For Mara and Tom

Contents

4. The Way the Blackbird's Song

5. Outside the School of Theology

MAYBE JUST ELEPHANTS

MAYBE JUST ELEPHANTS

Maybe Just Elephants

I'll never hunt with Hemingway, watch
the cautious feet of elephants move slowly over
the Serengeti, or hear the deep roar of lions shudder
dusty trees. I'd like to be one of those
white people with big tents and windup
Victrolas and cold gin. I'd smoke Lucky

Strikes even though I don't smoke and I'd fly
there in a two-seater biplane even though
I don't like to fly. I forgot to mention the quiet
native porters. Tent sides breathing gently
in the hot breeze. At midday there's a stillness
inside so large it presses against you, wants you

to submit to sleep or sex, it doesn't care which.
I'm not sure if it's the safari or only the tents I desire.
Tents that smell like boy scouts or wild yellow
flowers that grow by August roads, like dry
lightning. Tents big enough to hold trapeze artists, trick
ponies, tattooed ladies, dancing elephants. Me.

Sitting in the shade,
listening to the Victrola,
talking about elephants.
Maybe just talking.
Maybe just elephants.

Taiko Drummers

Feudal Japan was not all sword
play and fans. On stage here, women hiss
a command and the rhythm
changes. More. More.

Three men lean back
from their drums to pound with more
strength, beat with more
leverage. Like warriors

from another world, they transfix
with straight forward stares.
More. More. I wonder what they'd be like
in bed. Not the man with hard arms

and cruel mouth. The one whose eyes
close, whose face shows agony
and bliss. They pound.
Stop. Increase tempo. Pound.

Stop. More, more. I want this
to end. I want to know
how far it can go. The women
beat small drums. They smile.

I feel drums on the tight skin
of my chest. More.
More. My cells arrange
to match the beat—more

simple and more wild.
Sweat shines on
the drummers, slides down my back.
This demand cannot be satisfied

by dancing, it wants
surrender. Abandon. A fist
against the heart.
Then silence.

Today the Clouds

Today the clouds race   across
the foothills like a herd
of horses   snorting vapor
    from black nostrils
        chasing
    the grass   before them

        They pull
darkness   behind them   autumn's last
hours   rush   down the creekbed
with the leaves   So many
    short days to live through
        Driving

to see you I passed   one brown spotted
appaloosa   running   beside the canyon
    that curves along the road near
Athena   On the hillside five
    quarterhorses stood chest deep   in tall
    grass but she   ran   alone

    tail twisting   like willow whips
    hooves   tearing dust   Please
    touch me   like that
    Like cloud
        like wind
        like thunder

Going Over Emigrant Pass

The tamaracks have changed to yellow without me
noticing   Past Boiling Point I think of you
            and again as I look over   the ridge
near Deadman's Pass   on the other side of the Blues
                        Where I live

there are no empty spaces   I've been everyplace
I can see   In the Powder River Valley   wind
    tears at the sagebrush   tumbleweed rambles
past a mining camp   birds fly   through

an empty church   That whole world stands naked
without   memories to soften the Wallowas'
rough edges   I feel a constriction of heart
    call it loneliness   or fear   Coming back

home   I drink truck stop coffee   look
at the yellow hills   where even now you may be
    walking or   sleeping   or singing
under this trembling sky   No such thing
as a straight line or solid object   we are
                        transparent as fire

At Nehalem

At Nehalem the fog is like a secret
everyone knows. It crawls in
from the oyster beds,
but even the hot black coffee at the cafe
won't wake it up.
It drifts along past the basket weaver's shop,
up the hill to the winery,
where it gets lost
in the rhubarb wine
and is uncorked on Christmas,
a thousand miles away.

Dimension

Say we're on Star Trek and Picard says
We are approaching the Octaran Dimension.
What do you think? Someplace where
the number eight figures importantly
in the local mythology. And why not,
it has a nice shape, you can ice skate
in it and if you turn it sideways, it means
infinity. In the Octaran Dimension, spiders
are revered. Octopuses and scorpions, too.
The people there have just four digits,
like cartoon characters. On their eighth
birthday, Octaran children are given eight
notes to sing, on their sixty-fourth,
Octaran grandparents are honored
with fireworks. Every Octenium they
fear the Dimension will collapse.
Some menace bigger than the Enterprise
will land and attack their eight-sided cities,
but it never happens. Say we're on
the Enterprise. Say the next Dimension
is through that wormhole. Say Octaran.
Say you love me.

Watching the Big Top Go Up

If we get there real early
while the air is still cool
we can see the elephants do the slow dance
raising those poles. They remind
me of a bulldogging horse
who knows more about rope
and patience than her cowboy ever will.
If you look in their tiny eyes
they seem to be pondering you.
They say if I only had hands
and a bony structure in my mouth
that would let me speak,
I wouldn't be doing manual labor.
Out on the savanna, their heads
echo subsonic songs that travel
like telephones so I think they know
when the men are coming with their black guns
and saws to harvest ivory.
And there they may ponder, too,
why they have those big feet and toenails
and they're probably happy for the demise
of umbrella stands. They might tell stories
of the old days when the world
seemed as big as Africa and the mothers
were pleased to nurse more sons.
Their small-eared cousins prance

like bloated can-can girls,
then they build a pyramid
of preposterous cheerleaders.
Like the pony steps backward
to tighten the noose on the steer
the hunters inch closer
to a big-tusked male or
caught in a web of canvas and rope
the elephants create their own display case,
acrobats fly with no wings,
clowns don't even smile under their makeup,
the tattooed lady snores in the semi, tomorrow
circus, clowns, cowboys and elephants will all be gone.

A Conjunction of the Wild

As a child I thought trees made
the wind by the furious fanning
of their branches. They live together
in sociable clumps, gathered
at the river, or they stroll

in pairs down parkways.
All my life I have wished I could
join their communion—they beckon
with their many arms, but I cannot
decode their messages. What must time

be like, measured in circles, rooted
to one spot? I look at water pouring
over concrete spillways, under
the shade of sumac, cottonwood and
locust, a conjunction of the wild

and the constructed. I'd like to follow
the stream back deeper to a primeval
world where language is all
noun, where thought is a breeze
on my shoulderblade and no knife

can dissect structure from meaning.
Where the slow swirl of a maple seed
or the hard fall of an apple is punctuation.
Where swallows graph the secret poetry
of trees across the sky.

LAKE WATER LIES

LAKE WATER LIES

Lake Water Lies

Lake water lies still and smooth, I can feel
        it, like when someone I love
is in the next room of a quiet house. Sunset here,
        the creeks slide like mercury.
If they could escape the canyons,
        spread over dry ridges, rest
a while, they'd tame this wild land,
        but they hardly linger on their way
to the river. Lakes never run away.
        These quixotic creeks twist
like spiraled snakes. I don't remember lakes
        until afternoons like today when I wake
to the smell of reluctant rain.
        For a moment I think I feel someone
moving in the next room. If I look
        out the window I'll see a wooden dock
stretched across dark water, hear
        the sigh of boats tethered near the shore.

Windust on the Snake

At night the train sounds
comforting, a human presence
in a prehistoric land.
I wake to see running lights of barges,
the syrup slow pushing of the tugs
through these black canyon walls
that confine a river
on a river
in a river.
Before I went to bed
that air-conditioned tourist boat whizzed by
carrying strangers from Seattle, New York, Montana,
who will never touch the shore, feel
the heat or smell the sage dry air.
But this morning holds stillness
as if silence could break
or sound shatter
water's thin skin
wrinkled by the feet of a goose.
The sun inches down into the canyon,
warming basalt.
Under the trailer I spot that slow unwinding
forked tongue tasting a long hiss.
The flat arrowhead
still keeps on coming, four feet long
and diamond backed, tail broken,
no rattle, he moves

like a magic spell unbraiding through the grass.
Stop it square to ask a question, it coils
ready to pounce spit silent death in its fangs.
We stand locked
in an understanding lovers would envy
until I back away
and he sidewinds down to the sand.
                    I look at the river's slow
west winding and wish
we had taken its rattle
instead of its bite.

Memaloose

Even when I'm dead I want to feel
this fierce wind tear words
from my mouth. It rattles
the black branches like bones,
beats the river into frenzied

waves that strive against
the current, pulls my hair.
I raise my hands
into the spirits who haunt

this place, feel them slide
through my fingers,
push my breath back
into my chest. I'm still

writing my story between
two parentheses, still sleep
in a bed of sparks, my hands desire
the sacrament of the body.

That island is too barren
for the living and the dead
have sunk beneath the dam.
When I'm ready, I'll pile my canoe

with paintings and pens, my blankets
and books, push off from Two Sisters
at midnight and by dawn find
my way to Memaloose. Today

my hair flies through air
the color of leaves ripped
from those twisted trees.
But my eyes, resisting
the current, are the color of waves.

Toboggan

It's up there, in the rafters
of my garage, a reclining
question mark. A man might give you
diamonds or a ring, something
you can fit in a jewelry box,

but Minnesota gives you toboggans.
As oldest child I'm doomed to drag
it through my life and share
it not just with my children,
but nieces, nephews, neighbors

who've never ridden its slippery curves.
It's one of those things
that requires no skill or grace,
just brute bravery and substance.
We'd stand together at the top

of the hill, stomp our feet, blow
on our hands, marvel at the tiny
people below, discuss the trees
and finally embark. It seemed

nothing bad could happen
when you were so closely comforted
by other bodies. I thought this
must be how cows feel, part of something
bigger that doesn't particularly need me

to keep going. I could drop dead
and no one would notice unless my body
got cold. But this, too, was the Minnesota
way—fit in, don't rock the boat or
make waves, just do your job and silently,

if possible. I tell my children all
they need to know. Lean into the turns.
If you see a rock or tree, don't be afraid
to fall. Drag the sled back up the hill,
stomp your feet and test your weight again.

Against the Lake

Against the lake I hear the shimmer
of loon call, imagine the red eye reflects
a bloody moon. This is the sound
Northern Lights would make

if they could sing, green
ululation, cold fire. The mystery
of water cannot even be understood
by canoe. Count the beads

that fall off the paddle, transform
into the necklace of the bird.
They have no clicking sound like pearls,
they are feather soft and light

around. They could be strung
for the fragrant neck
of a lover, they could fall from a paddle
or from the sky. Moccasins are not soft

enough to prevent crushing—I should wear
the lady's slipper, tread air. The path
the moon makes on the water recedes
endlessly before me. That hollow

sound is just the paddle against the side
of my canoe, it is not my heart
waiting for an answering drum, it is just
another hollow sound on water.

Hear it again, full of sadness,
like the loon. It has rhythm,
it is following the moon. Beads
gather on the paddle, drip down

along my arms and I can feel
water's dark mystery shimmer
on my face, then drench my neck
with feathers, with beads.

In The Gorge

The river is flat like steel and a raft of ducks
has settled in the shadow of the cliffs. This time

of winter the light is as weak as the cold is strong.
That's why I'm surprised

at the way sun defines the gray edges
of that cloudbank. It's just before sunset

and I'm coming home from Portland in a world
that creates itself as I drive.

On top of the plateau, the sky
is endless. This time of day

my car's shadow sweeps across the fields
like Grendel. The river,

the cliffs, the clouds, the field, disappear
behind me. Maybe my thoughts hold

that cloud together. It covers such a small
piece of sky. There was a man with me

for a while, beautiful as clouds, common
as sagebrush, cold as the light.

I sometimes think things
do not exist until I see them.

Listen. This time of day if we stop
you can hear a meadowlark even in winter.

Listen. This time of year silence is a steep cliff
falling into the still river. Listen. This time

what I'm saying is meant for you. Listen.
This time.

Tonka

This is the lake I was born
beside, my first memory
of wind and whitecaps.
At night the smell of water

would divide around my head,
invite drowning. Flat black
snappers mudslide to shore,
their sharpened jaws

a warning. I watched
a dragging, held my breath
against the fear of bloated
flesh caught in a net,

waiting for the body to fly
up when dynamite pounds
water. Blue is not always
a peaceful color. Skulls must drift

like seashells trailing green
tangled hair. Those mounds
on shore are sacred, we plowed
around them, planted yellow corn.

What I learned from canoes
is the strength of ribs,
how they hold air, how emptiness
can carry and be filled

with life. If loons and heron
can balance over this cool
water, I can find a place
to breathe in my dry land.

3

SKYROCKET ROAD

SKYROCKET ROAD

Skyrocket Road

It starts out rutted
but full of hope,
climbing to where hawks circle
fenceposts, grasshoppers whirl dust.
The farmhouse is gone.
A root cellar remains,
its door closed
on an underground world.
The squeeze chute leans
against itself; the watering trough
is dry, like the well.
The hawks circle round again, lifted
by the hot wind that combs
the wheat. If you broke down
up here, you'd have to wait
for harvest.

He Was Not My Husband Then

He was not my husband
then, but I wanted him
to be. Watching him climb
those apple trees, smiling

with his white teeth and all
that curly black hair, who
wouldn't. He was so careful then,
never bruised one. Always got

the bonus for bins that don't
have culls. I drove to Chelan,
past the lake, imagined my life
as a fruit tramp, living

in the Plymouth or those tumble-
down cabins, it sounded good.
Almost. His mother said picking
cherries was her favorite part

of life. I even liked
his dog. He convinced me
to climb the tree, in spite
of my fear of ladders.

I strapped on the harness
and climbed into the greenery,
smiling down at him. Reaching
for apples, each one adding

weight, bending me, canvas
pouch swelling like pregnancy.
I could see the gray backbone
of the Cascades reflected

in water, fluttering
under the wind. Like ghost
mountains, or memories
of mountains, waving goodbye.

Swans in Montana

Driving back from Minnesota that year
I felt my life as big as Montana.
Telephone poles rushing up and back,

herds of pronghorn melting
into creek canyons and hawks
gusting through thin blue air.

Like those swans we saw floating
a reed-green pond, using the Bighorns
as their backdrop. We flew

by them, and hardly noticed
how their white wings matched
the snow that curved down glaciers.

The Bitterroots were not as bad
as we expected, Lolo not as high,
then suddenly the hills

of the Palouse dipped
toward home. I thought
we'd always be graceful,

expansive, white wings bursting
into the big western sky,
like swans in Montana.

One Night Driving

One night driving with the man who was my husband,
looking for his brother's house, a child's birthday celebration.
My mother-in-law in the back seat, worrying her gift
will not be accepted. We're near

the Hanford Reservation, on the Columbia River. Years
later we learn of the experiments with radiation.
By then my mother-in-law is dead of bone cancer.
It was near Christmas. It was dark. We crossed the green

bridge at Sacajawea, then the blue bridge at Kennewick,
took a wrong turn somewhere and ended
up in Howard Amon Park. How can I describe the black
river, my mother-in-law's fears, the fight
with my husband that hung in the air?

How can I describe
the boats, outlined in Christmas lights, that paraded, silently,
down the river? Or, later, the party, the cake, the candles
and singing in the dark. How can I define Christmas
or family, worry, or happiness, or even lost?

90 Days Same As Cash

Lying on credit applications works
and so does my new dishwasher.
I marked boxes for all the major
credit cards, Visa, American Express,
MasterCard and where it said other
I wrote Sears. On the commercial
there's a girl talking on the phone
and the dishwasher's running and
she's kinda pushing her hair
back from her face, smiling. That's
the one I got, the quiet one.
It has an adjustable top rack so easy
to wash canning jars, which in a way
could save me money, making my own jam
and grape juice. The salesman said
it has a garbage disposal
that could grind bones, you see
why I had to have it. Eight hundred
a month is not enough and I think
my five grand fellowship will disappear
as fast as the half-gallon of ice cream
I bought last night. So when the form
said monthly salary, I said two
grand and what the hell I've been there
five years. It said I don't have to include
money I get from my ex unless I want
to so I figure I'll make it a supportive
amount to make up for all the women who don't

count it. And I own my home, at an attractive
mortgage rate. As I wait for the fax
to come back, I expect to be nervous
but it's not as if I'm robbing a bank,
I just want some fucking credit
for what I've done, is a dishwasher
too much to ask? They deliver free,
they tell me, but installation costs me
forty bucks.

Looking at *Esquire*

I stare at the pages
trying to translate what I see
into the men I know.
I want to flip
casually through these pictures
and know what they mean.
There must be some code.
I know these ads are not you
but it seems you have a watch
like one of these
they call a chronograph.
You have slacks
like some of these,
and you're young and strong
like this impossibly groomed
volleyball team posed
before the net. In the front
of the magazine the torso
of a man lies in foamy surf
that exudes the fragrance
of herbs and ambergris,
but you smell like soap
and your own skin.
The cars they sell are black
or red, elegant
or fast, this is not
the magazine of the safe

or the station wagon.
What makes me sad
is the longing I feel.
Not for the beautiful men
or clothes, money or cars,
but somehow sad
to know I can't be
your buddy, your brother,
your partner,
your twin.

I Kicked That Habit Too

He blows in on a smile
and the smoke of his last cigarette.
You have to be close to smell
and then it's like something personal
between us.
I still crave nicotine
so I inch closer.
Legs sprawled, his head leans
in my direction, I think
he may rest on my lap.
There's the way he makes
a space in his chest,
a C, for me to read in
my head tucked
almost under his chin
like a father
or a tent.
I realize I miss protection
or safety, comfort—
things men can offer.
I want to crawl inside
warm, smell cigarettes,
feel laughter ripple your shirt
and maybe fall
asleep while you read.

Thousands of Silver

Walking alone, I feel the cyclone
sound of wings on my back,
then over my head—pushing

upward. The snake-curved neck
and broken broomstick
legs of a prehistoric bird

who is just another fisherman.
He picks his way daintily, from rock
to rock, but his eye is not the eye

of a ballerina, more like a hawk,
and his technique—relentlessly
successful. His wings fold fog

like great gauze fans, measure
rain with thousands
of silver feathers.

Looking Backward

I've worn cologne scented by a thousand
white flowers, grown my hair, cut, bleached
and dyed it, tried better elocution, listened
to NPR so I could talk about what
the UN ought to be doing, and nothing,
or no one has looked better to me
than a hot fudge sundae on a Saturday

night. I'm sorry. I hate to say that,
especially when I look at my thighs,
but I've had about a hundred
dates since my divorce and the only guy
who asked me about me was gay.
What does that say? I get lonely. I miss sex.
Today I was driving to College Place

and light was falling at a slant like just before
sunset, only it lasted all afternoon.
Maybe it was field dust from harvest,
or smoke from Oregon forest fires.
Maybe something more mysterious.
You can't teach at an apocalyptic college
in eastern Washington, on the edge

of a nuclear desert, and not start worrying
the weather means more than weather.
Times like this I wish I believed
in God or believed, the way I used to,
that everything works out
in the end. Looking backward
at my bookshelf, I have three

volumes of Chekhov, two
of Chandler, one
of Carver.
Boom.

4

THE WAY THE BLACKBIRD'S SONG

THE WAY THE BLACKBIRD'S SONG

The Way the Blackbird's Song

My days are orderly as tombstones
at Arlington, soldierly rows of identical white
slabs. But between the long parentheses

of my life I had hoped to avoid
this regimented order. The Dixie cemetery
has a more natural symmetry, angels have fallen

as often as they've flown off with the souls
of children who would be gone by now
anyway. It's surprising how many dead people

I had forgotten. Markers lay face down in the dirt,
marble ornaments like cannonballs rest beside
the graves, weeds grow tall until Memorial Day.

I know I shall lie here with the Lambs and Laidlaws,
my pioneering ended in the Blues. Perhaps someday
the pattern will soothe me, or I'll find new geometries

in the curve of earth. The way my children
break the smooth expanse of sky. The way
the blackbird's song defines the air.

More Blue

I gave him blue
flowers, the only way I knew
to let him see
me, they had green

leaves like daggers
or Japanese silk
screens and they open
in the morning, more blue,

and close each evening,
twilight, when the sky
gets purple. One star hangs

against the foothills
like diamond, they
stretch their backs

into the moon
rise, then disappear
like dreams. More blue

than the river carrying
salmon, than the frost
that grows on grapes or drapes

windows in the night
before a snow.
I would give him sky,

singing, drenching
rain for tears, I'd heal
every wound with silence
and cobwebs, slow time's

ticking hands to the deep
drum of heartbeat, wait
with him till morning, past
the daggers for more blue.

You Paint

You paint. I'll watch. We don't have
to even talk, or I could tell a story.
You don't have to listen. I could tell
about a long time ago before I lived here or

about when I was married or I could tell
one that you're in. You decide. Maybe
I'll just sit, look at the clouds
and the yellow hills out the window. Drink

some tea. I remember one time I was walking
with you and it seemed you forgot
I was there. Remember? Maybe not.
Then one time I got mad and made you run

to stay with me. You remember that.
When you said you could not go
further I wanted to test you, but something
in your helplessness, like a battered

moth or an iris bent over its stalk,
stilled me. As we crossed
the bridge, my anger dropped into the dark
creek. Sweat cooled me off. I remember

before I met you I climbed the steep
trail beside the Wallowa to those rocks scattered
next to the falls. From there the lake is not
much bigger than a silver earring. You know

the place. I could not see
anyone for miles. I lay down
in the sun and watched clouds walk
by. I remember that. You paint.

Proof

Consider the following. You are here
with me. Across the table or
across the room, or across
my body, you are here. And your value
to me is not absolute,
it keeps increasing.
Maybe someday you'll calculate
how thought changes what it considers.
Till then the longing
that brought you
seems eternal.

Consider the possibility I exist
because you need me or you need me
because I exist. I don't mean to frighten you.
If we transpose pronouns, substitute terms,
the answer is the same, I need you too.
The constant in our equation is a concept
for which we have no measure
beyond abundance. What other explanation
can there be? I doubt our attraction is random.
This should be easy for you.
Facts demonstrate tendencies, interpretation
may be the realm of divinity. We could
roam beyond the limit
of this dusty world.
It has been shown.

You Can See How

You can see how this time
of year this time of day
the sun sets south of the Gap

and how it turns
these hills the color of salmon
every night you can see the way

the leaves lie yellow scattered
where deer walk and snow laces
the space between them

the trees reach over
the path and you can see how
the light slants in beneath

branches like fire not even
a bird has disturbed this orange
trail the creek has not

frozen yet hills hunch beside
it like rough dogs I stop
to look at a stile that climbs over

nothing the fence is a barbed
wire memory you can see
how I look at you and wonder

if the way is clear this golden
light cannot remain our footsteps will
surely change the snow.

Numb

It's strange that absence of feeling
in a certain area should be called numbness—
when the lack is so profoundly felt. Driving my
car, cutting an onion, my body is comfortable,
invisible, almost, except where it is numb.
Two fingers and part of my palm
are the focus of all my awareness. There's
a coldness there, and the other impairment,
of movement. Absence of pain would
seem a good thing, but bad things happen
when you're numb. Taking rice from the steamer
I couldn't feel the burn soon enough.

I have been places where for too long
it hasn't snowed enough to fill a lake. Smooth
and level except when the wind blows, it's only
around the edges things look a little different. No
trees or grass where these should be, only cracked
mud. You have to live there to know the deeper
changes. Fish that died, great flocks of Canada
geese that never migrated home.

That's how it's been for me. My right arm still
looks the same, spattered with light
brown freckles, ending in the familiar hand,
it seems no different than its left-side twin. But I am not
as strong. And what I mean to say
is when you were here I could
compensate. Mostly I don't
think anyone can see I have changed unless
they notice how I hold my arm close
to my chest, how I step back from handshakes.
It's the deeper changes I fear. Muscles
shrinking slowly. Years without rain.

Apparition

The light falls from these windows
milky and thin and outside bare
branches seem to scratch
against the hills. Sunday morning
light. The fire is yellow

and the paint yellow, I am floating
through yellow trying to get
warm. Maybe there was a time before
you, before this yellow day, before.
I feel weightless blue. Light

falls on my hand warm, a force
that could move those hills, shape
rocks, bend the creek closer
to my side. I see my four horsemen
riding closer, out there

on the ridgeline. They never
speak, they tremble
like the grass. I see shadows
through their hair. I watch you paint
the outline of a silent sky.

Learning to Weave

Every basket I make has threads
of my hair twined through it, my DNA
encoded in the weft, like fingertip swirls
show where we may have clung

to the Milky Way before our hands were pulled
loose to wrap around a mother's breast.
It's that shape we keep repeating.
I sit on the floor and arrange my baskets

in a small solar system. The red one
can be Mars. The one with stripes is Saturn.
In this one I weave sky, white clouds, blue
rivers, silver mountains and a red thread

of sorrow. Maybe this is how planets
are made. And families. Stories weave
us together then spin us into the world
until we can no longer tell the creation

from the creator. I want to make
my basket strong enough to hold rocks,
carry water, hide secrets. Like fingers
braid lives together, if only for an instant.

OUTSIDE THE SCHOOL OF THEOLOGY

OUTSIDE THE SCHOOL OF THEOLOGY

Easter Eggs

In the darkest part of winter,
after Christmas, before Lent,
the Ukrainian ladies would come to Dayton's.
They sat on high stools with gooseneck lamps,
beeswax, some kind of stylus,
ink, eggs and dye.
They brought light.
Each egg a marvel,
no pattern, no plan,
no two alike.
I wished I had a heritage that had produced
something more beautiful than *lefse*.
The eggs were hope.
They were faith in the spring to come.
They were belief in beauty
and order, regularity.
While we suffered through Lent,
suffered through each others' sacrifices,
the eggs lay on the mantle,
promising resurrection.

Singing the Mozart Requiem

Like 97 beautiful crows,
shadow beads of a necklace
that stretches through the dark

past the cold Gothic arches.
Our iridescent feathers
tuxedo-best, velvet-dress

plumage, catch the fire
of these windows
where the ministry of Jesus

is as simple as a child's
picture book. High above,
the moon hides

behind a rag of cloud,
the steeple points at God
knows what, stars revolve

in space like the wheeling
of crows. The church swallows
us one by one, as death

will do, my breath wreathes
my hair like a soul
departing. Who knows

what brings this fierce
and sudden joy?

Any Sunday

Any Sunday you can find me
here, under the cottonwoods
near the VA water tower.
I come to listen for church
bells over the valley

and the rustle of leaves.
There's also a redtail I like
to watch sail out over
the trailer court that huddles

next to the highway. Today
the mountains tease behind
white vapor, like a name
I can't remember. I can't think
how I ever got to a place

where I have to talk to trees.
I want to fly over the valley
screaming the way she
hangs against the sky, waiting

for the next updraft. Or diving,
striking fire from my wings. Some
silken jess of wind, tangled
in my fingers, ties me to the earth.

Outside the School of Theology

Outside the School of Theology, an article
from *The Sun* is taped to the wall.
"Adam & Eve's Skeletons Found—
in Colorado!" The photo shows two

skeletons lying rib by rib. Their knees bend in
the same direction, Adam's in the space
behind Eve's. His right arm—humerus, radius,
and ulna—stretches beneath Eve's head,

her pillow for the night, for forever.
I'm glad to see Adam didn't hold a grudge
about the apple. Of course, a lot has happened
since then. Cast out of the Garden, they

wandered for a while, took up farming.
Maybe when Cain was grown
they bought a Winnebago and criss-crossed
America, sent postcards to the grandkids.

"Overheated in a godforsaken desert,"
Adam would say. "Think I'll call it
Death Valley." He was still in charge
of naming. Finally one day,

they got tired. Or maybe they thought
they had wandered back to Eden.
I've felt that way, in Colorado.
So many years had passed, they had

forgotten about the snake. Eve's
days of childbirth were long
gone and Adam was done scraping
his living from the thin soil of Goshen.

They lay down. They looked
at the stars. They were so old
they no longer thought they could
distinguish good from evil.

They said their nightly prayer
for Abel. Eve said, "Adam, it's time
to go home." And Adam said,
"All right, dear. Good night."

Beyond the Fire

Beyond the fire darkness
moves always one step
away. It surrounds but never
quite swallows me or the cottonwoods

who gather at the river turning
dusty palms to the wind.
I'm listening to the rocks
under water turning slow circles

like stars. The fire builds
black walls and sparks
explode into the Ponderosa,
but I don't see them pinwheel

into night. I walk
to the cottonwoods, twist
their knuckled twigs
in my fingers, lay

my face against rough
bark. When at last the moon
crawls over the mountain,
my shadow is my twin, my substance

as thin as those heart-
shaped leaves. I know
my way. The path worn
by elk and horses, bear padding

softly after salmon. Like Jacob
I'll use a rock for a pillow,
all night wrestle this black
angel, my shadow in the moon.

Bones

Walking through this meadow
between two low hills, I can see
the battle, but not the ghosts
of warriors who haunt
the creekbed. As if I could

see the boy who jumped
off the cutbank to warn
the people, and Eagon retreating,
they seem like faces

I know. Grasshoppers click
in the grass, foxtails scratch
my ankles. Near blackberries
we pick stories, thorns

and fruit entwined. I keep
thinking of those horse and elk
ribcages rising like small cathedrals
or rotted ships. They rest

on this shore nudged up almost
to the mountains where the grass
waves yellow in the hot wind.
Words connect like vertebrae

linking rib to rib. If
I press my backbone into the earth,
its trail will remember
my story. I dig a handful of dirt
and smell the blood of horses.

Why Mormons Think They're Special

Last summer I drove to Arizona as if
I was trying to find my way
home. Slept by the side of the road, drew
pictures in the dust—a simple highway
life. Sleeping bag, coffeepot, ice chest.
Toothbrush, washcloth, comb. In Utah

I could understand why Mormons
think they're special. I would too, if God
gave me a country where angels and gargoyles
decorate arches as graceful as Chartres. And no rose
window could compare colors with the fractured
landscape. Red rock, green pine, blue sky
deeper than pain. I decided to angle

into Colorado, dig around for the root
of America. The night before Mesa Verde
I slept at the foot of a mountain outlined
in stars. All that country
I pulled around me and wore
like a ceremonial dress. I wanted it

the way I want food or sex. Sometimes
new landscapes satisfy desires
I didn't know I had. Maybe I was looking for God
or a way out, or a way into the grace
of cliff dwellings secured by mud
and faith between earth and heaven.

This Landscape

This landscape of rock cleft
river tugs at a damp place
in me. I cannot hold
the steep cliffs and petroglyphs,
only those rocks my legs

remember, climbing where
the mountains rise behind
me and the river turns
below. I drive through smoking

fields where fire prepares
dirt for spring. Dust
devils whistle me into the canyon.
Tonight I'll wear cinnamon and sage,
reflect fire, burn candles

on my windowsill as leaves
rattle to the ground. Outside
a moth beats against the light.
I turn in my bed to the moon,

just opening its aperture
over the ridge. Dust and smoke
stain the air with their dark
scent, coyotes call across the canyon,
something flickers in

the weeds. The tapping
on the glass begins again. Shadows
rush over the hillside, pushing
the grass before them.

What Awaits Me

Maybe it's the rusting barge
abandoned in the river on its way
to Lake Washington that makes me think
something is going to happen,

perhaps it's the turbulence that lifts us
into more thin air, but the plane
approaches the runway,
the landing gear drops

with a thud and suddenly we are airborne
again, rushing upward over the hangars,
back through the clouds,
dipping our wings over Mt. Rainier.

I do not pray. For perhaps the first time
in my sometimes superstitious life, I do not
knock wood or offer bargains
to God and I don't care that nothing

is probably what awaits me
on the other side. I don't think
about my lover, who I just left
in San Jose, or all the things

I haven't done.
All I regret is being late—
my children waiting
for an airplane that never

arrives. Lately I have become
painfully aware that my destiny
is often beyond my control. My neck
vertebrae have crumbled

like the mortar between old
bricks, and it occurs to me
what a mess my life would be
if we crashed and I survived. And yet

I walk constantly on a sea
of faith. For every self
important businessman who pushes past
me in the aisle, three strangers step

in to hand me my briefcase and carry
my bag. If I drop
a twenty-dollar bill, unknown hands
reach out to return it.

When the voice of the captain
explains that a Cessna broke down
on the runway and this is why
we have circled Seattle,

the desire to land in my home
state grips me, a fierce passion. Once again
we pass the rusting barge,
once again the crowded freeway

seems precariously close,
once again the prospect of coffee
in Seattle revives me, but this time
I know we will arrive safely.

Even so, with my good left hand,
I touch the window of the airplane,
offer it my frail human blessing and thank it
for its strong, man made wings.

Books distributed by Tsunami Inc.

Michael Finley, *Lucky You*, Litmus Inc., 1976, $5
Charles Foster, *Victoria Mundi*, Litmus/Smith, 1973, cloth $10
d.a. levy, *Collected Poems*, Druid Books, 1976, $10
Charles Potts, *How the South Finally Won the Civil War,*
  and Controls the Political Future of the United States, 1995,
  Tsunami Inc., cloth, 11 maps, index, 200+ works cited, $29
  100 Years In Idaho, Tsunami Inc., 1996, $10
  Loading Las Vegas, Current, 1991, a satiric novel, $10
  The Dictatorship Of The Environment, Druid Books, 1991, $10
  Lettered & signed cloth bound limited edition, $25
  Rocky Mountain Man, The Smith, 1978, $10
  The Opium Must Go Thru, Litmus Inc., 1976, $5
  Cover and illustrations by Robert McNealy,
  Quarter bound in leather sewn into boards by the author, $50
  A Rite To The Body, Ghost Dance, 1989, $5
Edward Smith, *The Flutes Of Gama*, Litmus Inc., 1976, $5
Stephen Thomas, *Journeyman*, Tsunami Inc., 1997, $15
Teri Zipf, *Outside the School of Theology*, Tsunami Inc., $10

Pacific Northwestern Spiritual Poetry, an anthology of 50 poets,
Tsunami Inc., edited with an introduction by Charles Potts, $20

The Temple, Gu Si, El Templo, an 80 page quarterly of poetry
in English with Chinese and Spanish poems along with English
translations: sample $5; Set of volume 1, 1997, issues 1-4, $20;
one year subscription, $20.

Tsunami Inc.
PO Box 100, WALLA WALLA, WA 99362-0033
<http://www.wwics.com/~tsunami>
<tsunami@wwics.com>